Darling 'Bec
Something
to remind you
of Melbourne
& all of us
Feb 2008
Lots of love
Dad,
Kate
& Evan xxx.

Australia In Focus

MELBOURNE & BEYOND

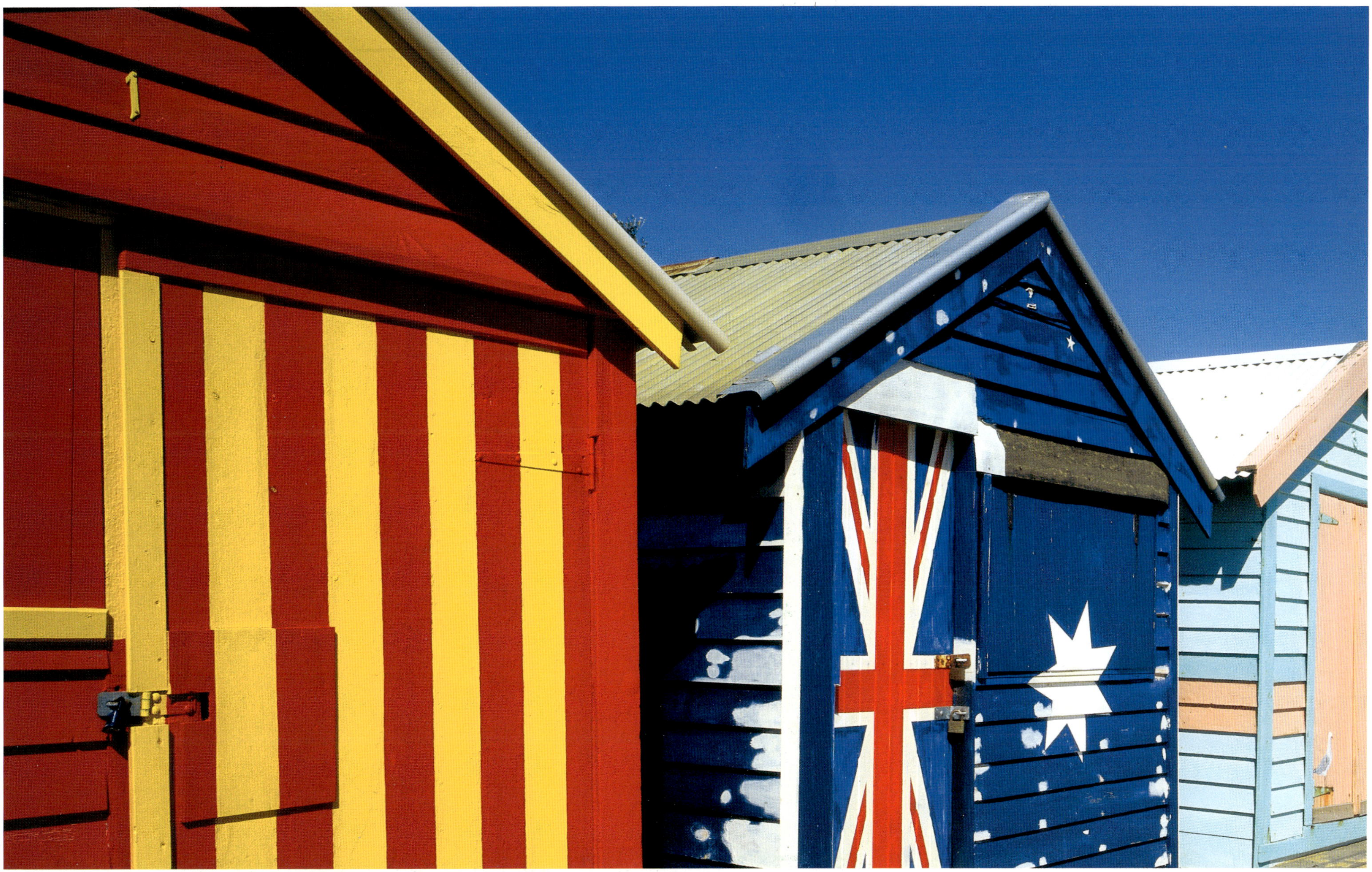

CONTENTS

Previous pages: *Twelve Apostles, Port Campbell National Park.*
Left: *Flinders Street Station, completed in 1910.*

INTRODUCTION

An important city by world standards, Melbourne, capital of the State of Victoria, has a wealth of natural and created beauty. The city's charm lies in its grace and spaciousness, its exciting diversity and its physical beauty. Its architecture is a stimulating mixture of old and new: beautifully aged nineteenth-century creations stand beside buildings of startlingly modern design.

Lush green parks and gardens linked by broad boulevards give breathing space to the tensions of closely built areas. Through the city, the Yarra River winds serenely to Port Phillip Bay, much of its course bordered by green spaces.

In 1835, the Aboriginal people who had lived along the banks of the Yarra for thousands of years allowed a group of settlers to found a village. Neither John Batman nor John Fawkner, rival founding fathers, could have foreseen its growth into today's bustling cosmopolis of more than three million residents.

Melburnians have eclectic tastes. Sport is as important to them as the arts and even the notorious weather does not deter them from making the most of public spaces and events. They eat well in the city's cafés and restaurants, which offer cuisine from around the world. They dress well in the creations of world-renowned couturiers. And they live well in one of the world's most liveable cities.

Melbourne is a city of style and sophistication. A variety of landscapes and lifestyles are to be enjoyed in the city and its surrounds. Quiet relaxation or nightlife excitement, classy hotels or quaint bush cabins, wild country or manicured gardens – whatever your heart desires is here.

Opposite: Prior to Port Melbourne, in the 1870s the Melbourne and Hobsons Bay Railway Company Pier stood on the site where Station Pier was constructed. Right: The modern city awakes behind the peaceful waters of Williamstown Harbour. Following pages: Melbourne glitters as night falls over the city.

MELBOURNE: A CITY OF HEART

Melbourne's pleasures are plentiful and diverse. Some, like the stately grandeur and beautifully preserved nineteenth-century architecture of its public buildings, are readily apparent. Others, like the city's exotic assortment of cuisine, art and entertainment may be concealed within the maze of lanes and alleys that are part of Melbourne's soul.

Like all great cities, Melbourne does not reveal itself entirely at first encounter, but retains a modest mystique and character all the more rewarding to those who seek it out. It is a city of many hearts – a natural wonderland of superbly designed gardens and parks; a modern international business centre; a vibrant hub of artistic achievement and one of the world's great sporting capitals.

Melburnian's pride in their city is not shouted out loud but finds expression in an inclusive, multi-faceted culture. When the residents do raise their voice as one it is likely to be in fervent support of Australian Rules football teams at the MCG, home to the 1956 Olympics and the XVIII Commonwealth Games. Fashion and dining are no less a passion.

Savour the city's sumptuous offerings on the re-born banks of the Yarra River, at Federation Square or in the sight of one of its glorious cathedrals. Or perhaps simply feast on nature's delights in Melbourne's magnificent parklands. This is a city that freely shares its copious gifts with guests and finds a permanent home in their hearts.

Opposite: *Strolling past graceful restored terraces.*
Above left: *Acland Street in St Kilda is renowned for its cake shops.*

Left: The commercial towers of Melbourne rise behind the
Royal Exhibition Building and Melbourne Museum.
Above: Urban motion outside Flinders Street Station.
Right: Eureka Tower rises 91 storeys over Southbank.

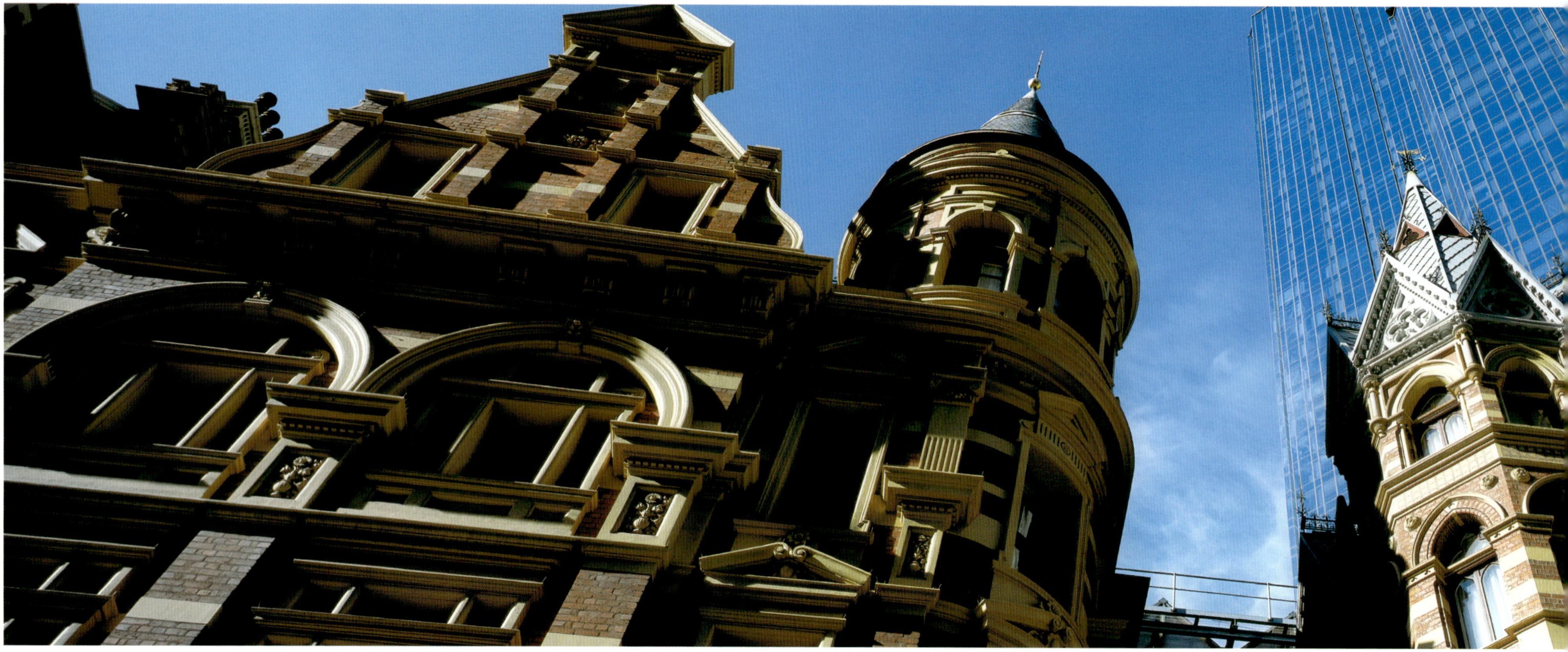

HOTEL
HOTEL WINDSOR

WINE MERCHANTS
McDonald's

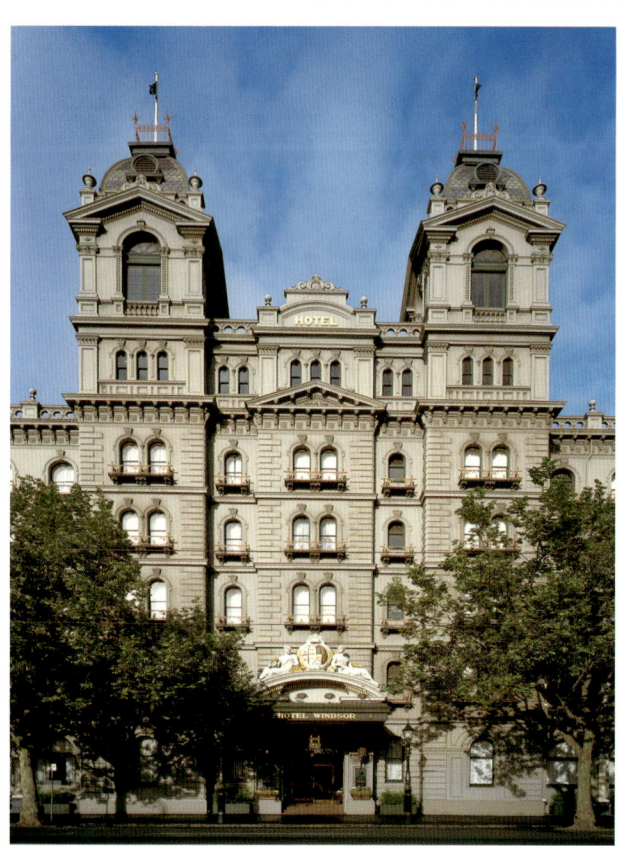

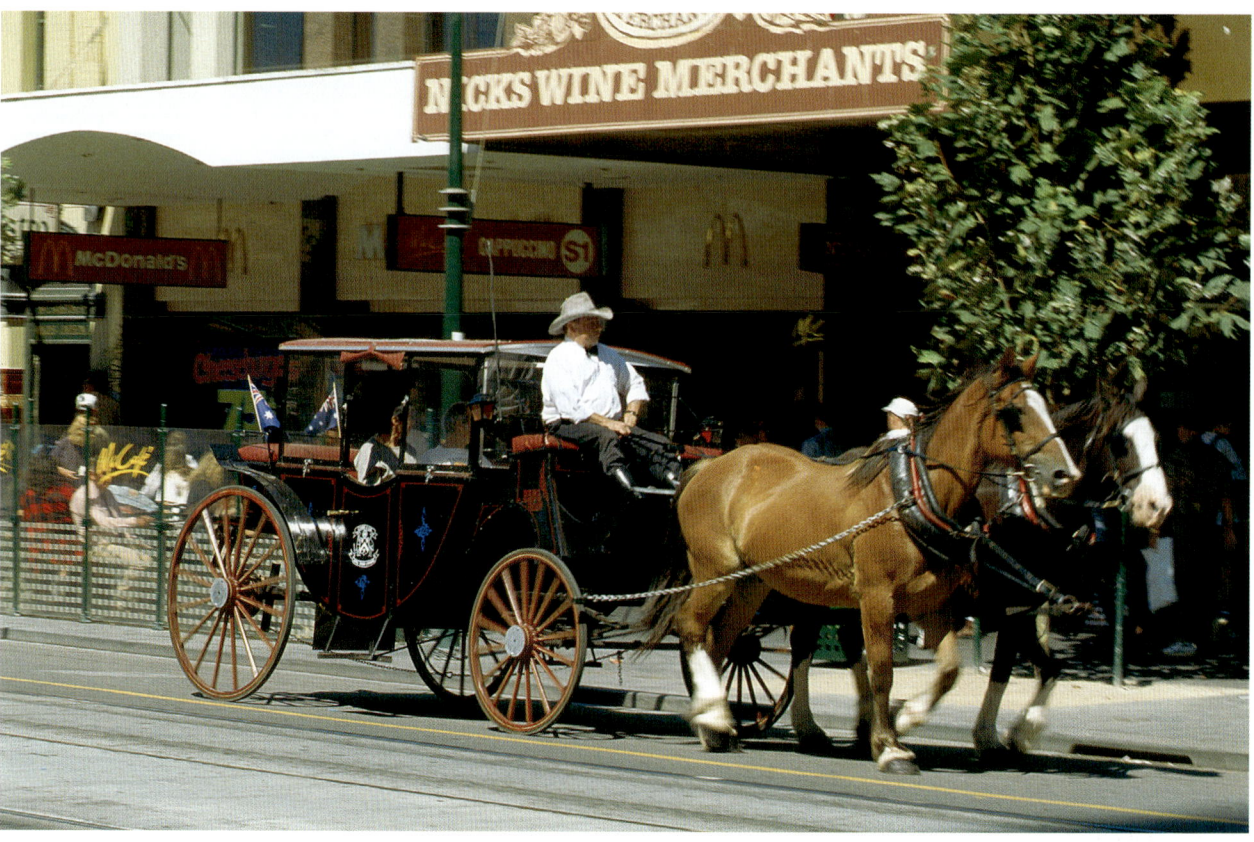

HISTORIC MELBOURNE

Melbourne, with its rich array of heritage buildings, is renowned as one of the finest examples of a Victorian city remaining anywhere in the world. These grand private, commercial and public structures were born of the wealth generated by mid-nineteenth-century booms in gold and wool.

The beautiful St Patrick's and St Paul's Cathedrals reflect this era of prosperity and provide classic examples of neo-Gothic architecture.

Upon the nation's Federation in 1901, prior to Canberra's conception, the Australian Federal Parliament was formally opened under the Great Dome of Melbourne's Royal Exhibition Building and sat in the Victorian Parliament House in Spring Street until 1927.

*Top: The intricate detail of St Paul's Cathedral contrasts with the city's sleek, modern towers. **Far left to right:** Hotel Windsor, built in 1883; a horse and carriage revive Melbourne's past in Swanston Street Walk; Como House at South Yarra is an elegant colonial mansion; the imposing entrance to Victoria's Parliament House.*

Left: Melbourne's beautiful red brick Public Baths sit on the corner of Victoria and Swanston Streets. *Above:* The soaring domed ceiling of the former Commercial Bank of Australia at 333 Collins Street, built in 1891. *Following pages:* One of Melbourne's famed trams passes another Melbourne transport icon, Flinders Street Station.

Elegant old churches grace Melbourne City. **Opposite:** St Patrick's Cathedral was completely restored in the 1990s to celebrate the centenary of its consecration.
Above left to right: Neo-Gothic detail and spires are a feature of St Paul's Cathedral on the corner of Swanston Street Walk and Flinders Street; the interior of St Paul's Cathedral.

Right: Originally built for the 1880 Victorian International Exhibition, the Royal Exhibition Building and surrounding Carlton Gardens are world renowned, having been inscribed on the World Heritage List in 2004.
Above, top to bottom: Hochgurtel Fountain; blooms and fountains adorn Carlton Gardens.

OLD MELBOURNE GAOL

Melbourne's bluestone gaol, built in 1842, is now a museum offering a chilling insight to early penal experience. Primarily housing short-term prisoners, the gaol's inmates included transported convicts, petty criminals and the condemned awaiting their fate. One hundred and thirty-five prisoners met their end here at the gruesome trapdoor gallows before the gaol's closure in 1929. They included Australia's most notorious bushranger, Ned Kelly, hanged on 11 November 1880.

During World War II, the gaol was re-opened and operated as a military detention prison. The existing building in Russell Street formed the north wing of a larger complex including warder's houses and a hospital. Visitors can venture along narrow walkways permitting access to the original cells and gallows landing. The gaol also presents theatrical re-enactments of events past and exhibits a unique collection of death masks, lashing triangles and cat-of-nine tails.

Left: *The Cell Block at Old Melbourne Gaol.*
Right: *The suit of armour that once protected Ned Kelly's brother, Dan Kelly.*

SHRINE OF REMEMBRANCE

Rising out of parklands on the fringe of Melbourne's city centre, this important memorial, opened in 1934, stands in perpetual tribute to those who served and those who died for their country in war.

The original design was the outcome of a competition won by two returned soldiers, Peter Hudson and James Wardrop, both architects. Its classical form is inspired by one of the seven wonders of the ancient world – the Mausoleum at Halicarnassus in Asia Minor. Following World War II, the forecourt and other memorials were added in honour of the fallen of successive generations.

At 11.00 a.m. on Remembrance Day, the eleventh day of the eleventh month each year, a ray of sunlight enters through an opening in the Shrine ceiling, passes over the Stone of Remembrance and illuminates the word "love". The Shrine is also the centrepiece of major annual commemorations marking Anzac Day on April 25.

Left: *The Shrine of Remembrance in the Domain Parklands.*
Right: *The Eternal Flame burns in front of the Shrine.*

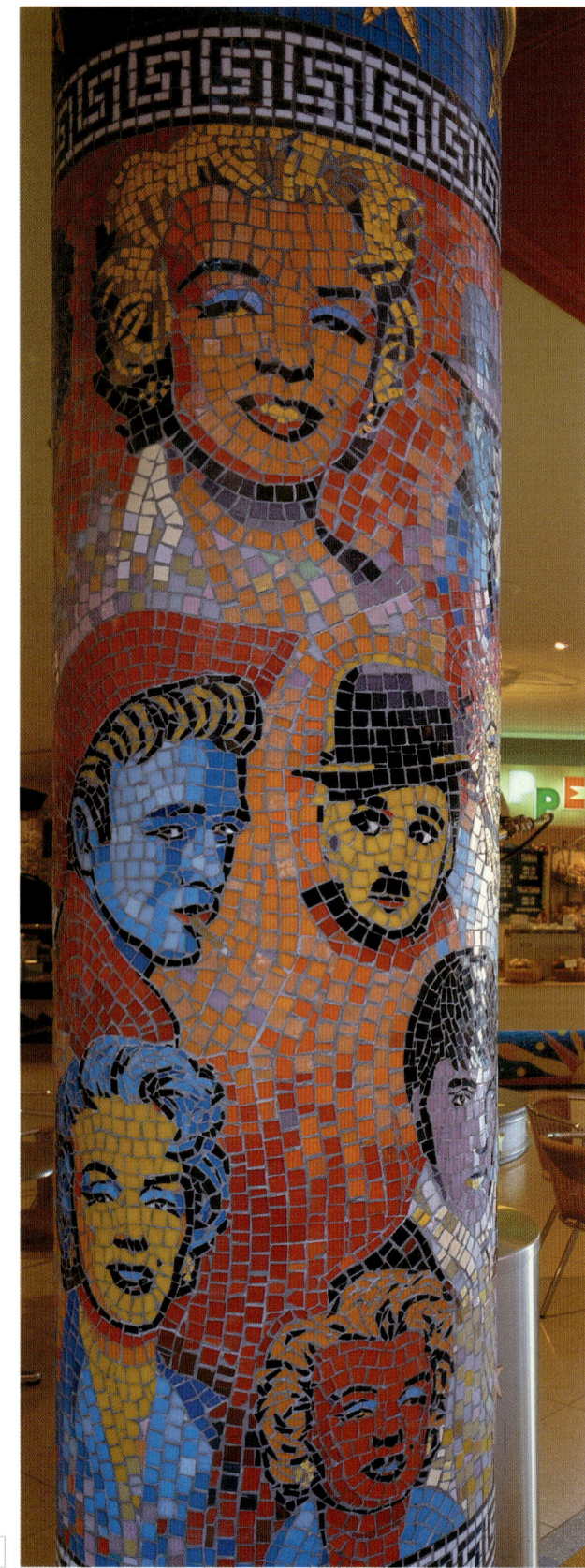

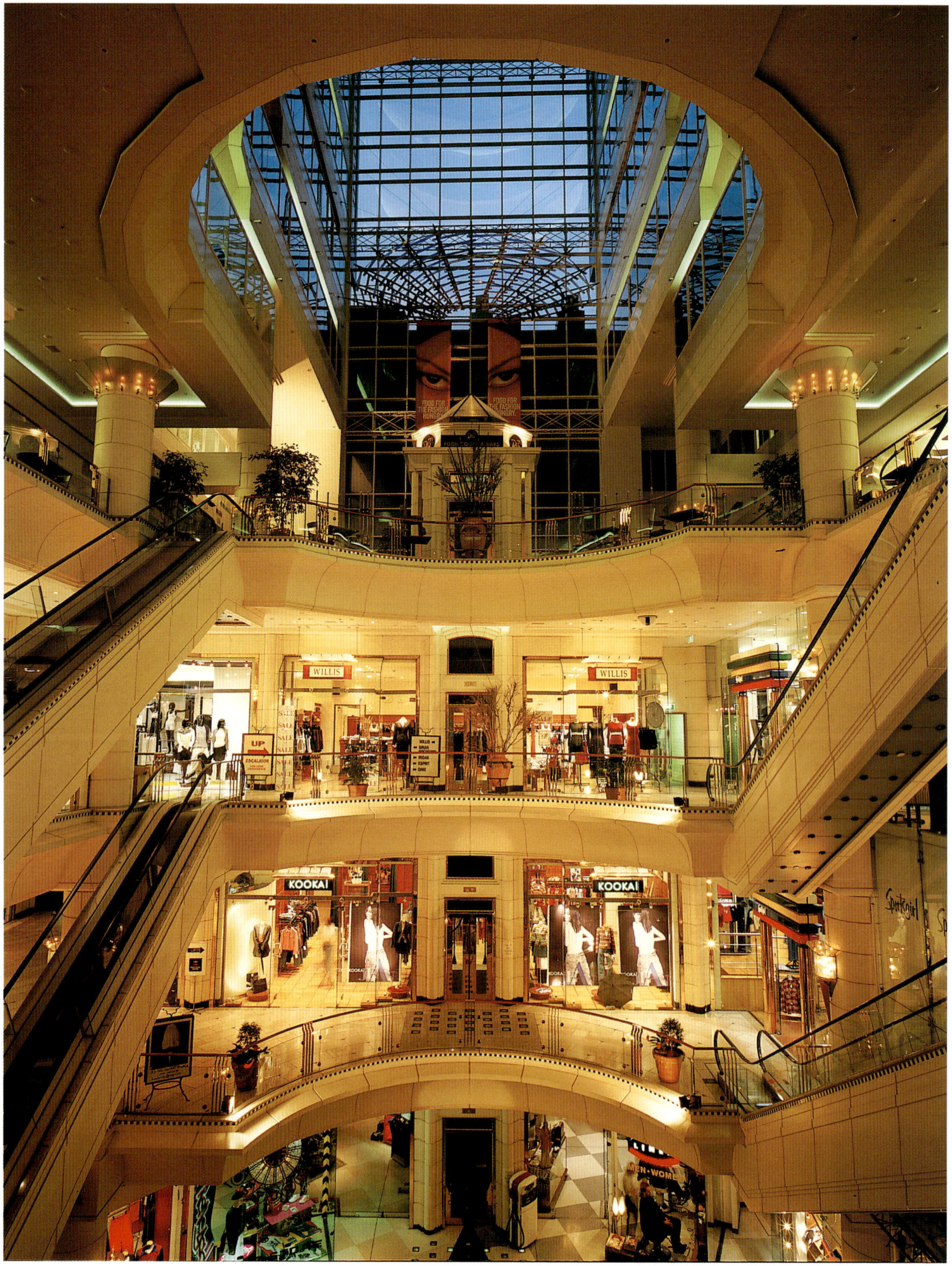
WILLIS
WILLIS
KOOKAI
KOOKAI

SHOPPING FOR ALL SEASONS

Melbourne offers an inviting shopping experience that ranges from tiny exclusive boutiques to multi-storey retail complexes. Within the city's network of arcades and lanes can be found stylish shops offering wares to suit all tastes. Melbourne Central, set around a historic Shot Tower, is a major indoor shopping plaza over an underground railway station. Beyond the city, the fashion conscious revel in the couture culture of Chapel Street at South Yarra, while Bridge Road, Richmond, is lined with fashion warehouses and designer outlets. Lovers of old wares find antique treasures in High Street, Armadale, or fossick for shabby chic in the retro bric-a-brac stores of Brunswick Street, Fitzroy.

Opposite from left: These colourful mosaics at South Yarra's Jam Factory feature twentieth-century movie greats; stylish retail stores beckon shoppers. Above: Royal Arcade, Australia's oldest retail arcade, houses some of the city's most elegant shops, guarded by statues of the fabled giants Gog and Magog.

Melbourne Museum

Located adjacent to the Royal Exhibition Building in Carlton Gardens, Melbourne Museum provides an enthralling and challenging perspective on natural sciences, Indigenous cultures, Australian history and cultural heritage. Opened in October 2000, the museum comprises spacious galleries and exhibition spaces including the Bunjilaka Aboriginal Centre, the Evolution Gallery and Children's Gallery. The 35-metre-high Forest Gallery is a living interpretation of Victoria's temperate forests incorporating nearly 8000 trees and plants and 20 different vertebrate species, including snakes, birds, fish and frogs. Melbourne Museum also frequently presents major international touring exhibitions.

Opposite: This 18.7-metre Blue Whale skeleton, preserved after its stranding near Lorne in 1992, greets visitors to the Melbourne Museum. ***Above and left:*** The modern forecourt and entrance to the Museum in Carlton Gardens.

VICTORIAN ARTS CENTRE AND NGV INTERNATIONAL

Melbourne has an international reputation for its nurturing and celebration of the arts. Each spring, the Melbourne International Arts Festival attracts some of the world's most talented artists. Throughout the year, Melburnians and visitors are drawn to the Victorian Arts Centre precinct to enjoy a range of theatre, dance and music. Below the landmark Arts Centre spire are gathered some of the city's finest performing arts venues including the Melbourne Concert Hall, the State Theatre, the Playhouse and the George Fairfax Studio. Behind a 15-metre-wide moat, the nearby NGV International, the National Gallery of Victoria, at St Kilda Road is dedicated to the exhibition of the Gallery's impressive international collection.

Left: *The spire above the theatre complex of the Victorian Arts Centre is dazzlingly dramatic at night.*
Above, left to right: *Promenade, Performing Arts Centre; Angel, by Deborah Halpern, in the moat at NGV International.*

FOOD AND FUN

Melbourne's many markets and specialist food stores overflow with a spectacular cornucopia of produce. A visit to the Queen Victoria Market is a journey through the colours and flavours of four seasons in one day. Here, at the largest open air market in the Southern Hemisphere, can be found culinary delights to make the most sophisticated gourmet's mouth water. At Prahran and South Melbourne, popular undercover markets offer everything from fresh food and flowers to clothing and books. While browsing, shoppers are often treated to colourful performances and entertainment from buskers, pavement artists and street parades.

These pages: *The Melbourne experience must include joining the crowds that throng to festivals, celebrations, markets and shopping precincts. Melburnians love to be out of doors and they love to shop. Buskers and street artists bring music and colour to the scene (be it the Moomba Waterfest, shopping at the market, or keeping up with the latest fashion) which showcases the best, most stylish and freshest of produce, products, ideas and talents.*

MELBOURNE ZOO

Spreading out across one of Melbourne's many green oases, just four kilometres from the city, Melbourne Zoo is Australia's oldest. Home to over 350 species, with a strong focus on conservation, the Zoo has been meticulously planned to provide its animals with surroundings closely resembling their natural habitat. This approach has led to unprecedented success in many of the Zoo's breeding programs, including the breeding in captivity of some of the world's most endangered species, such as the Lowland Gorilla. A magnificent example of the Zoo's attention to detail is the Trail of the Elephants, which accurately recreates the environs of a South-East Asian village on the fringe of the tropical rainforest. A historic menagerie exhibit provides visitors with an insight into how the conservation of animals has evolved over the past century.

Clockwise from top left, and opposite: Melbourne Zoo, in Parkville, provides a lush environment for its residents (some pictured opposite); students visit the Japanese Garden; the Zoo's Butterfly House. **Following pages:** *Government House and the Sidney Myer Music Bowl nestle amid the gardens skirting the city and the Yarra River.*

AT NATURE'S HEART

From Melbourne's beginnings, large tracts of public land were reserved for public gardens. Beside the Yarra are the manicured lawns and floral splendour of the Royal Botanic Gardens. In Fitzroy Gardens is Cook's Cottage, relocated from Yorkshire in 1933.

Opposite: A well-ordered and eye-catching bloom in Carlton Gardens. **Clockwise from top:** *Cook's Cottage; parks and gardens adorn the city.* **Following pages:** *Colourful floral displays and a classical-inspired sculpture in the Conservatory, Fitzroy Gardens.*

THE SPORTING CAPITAL

Sport in Melbourne is a year-round event. Melburnians' passion for a sporting contest is legendary, be it their beloved Australian Rules football, or Australia's most famous horse race, the Melbourne Cup.

In winter, tribes of football fans proudly don their favourite team's colours and flock to Melbourne's sporting epicentre, the MCG (Melbourne Cricket Ground). In summer, it is transformed into one of the world's great cricket arenas. The MCG is Australia's only stadium to host both the Olympic and the Commonwealth Games.

Opposite the MCG are Melbourne and Olympic Parks, more of Melbourne's great sporting venues. Rod Laver Arena is the international stage for one of the four Grand Slam tennis events, the Australian Open.

*Left: The Melbourne Cup, the "race that stops a nation" is run on the first Tuesday in November every year at Flemington Racecourse. **Right:** Melburnians are passionate about Aussie Rules. **Following pages:** Albert Park Lake and parklands, tranquil until the heady excitement of the annual Formula One Grand Prix.*

Albert Park Lake and surrounding parklands, set close to the city, have many moods. **Clockwise from top:** *Australian Formula One Grand Prix; a swan on Albert Park Lake; cycling in the park; lakeside jogging.*

LAKESIDE SPORTING FACILITIES AND GRAND PRIX CIRCUIT

A tranquil artificial lake formed by the excavation of lagoons in 1880, Albert Park Lake and its parklands are a focal point for recreational and sporting activity in Melbourne. Only three kilometres from the city, the environs boast walking, running and cycling tracks, sports ovals and boating facilities.

Each year the lakeside is spectacularly transformed to host the Australian Formula One Grand Prix, attracting international competitors and more than 300,000 spectators.

At the lake's south-west tip is the Melbourne Sports and Aquatic Centre, a principal events venue for the XVIII Commonwealth Games and the 12th FINA World Championships. Built to world-class standard, the Centre provides multi-function facilities for swimming, diving, water polo, basketball, badminton, table tennis, handball, volleyball and squash.

Above and left: The Melbourne Sports and Aquatic Centre at Albert Park Lake is one of the city's largest sporting facilities and plays host to a range of events.

49

MELBOURNE BY NIGHT

When evening falls, Melbourne promises a unique experience for all, from theatre and gourmet dining to the vibrant colour of Chinatown. The illuminated palatial facade of the Princess Theatre invites attendance at the musical productions now staged within. Later, an eclectic array of bars and clubs in the city's alleys and lanes cater to every taste.

Opposite: The Princess Theatre in Spring Street. **Clockwise from top left:** *Chinatown in Little Bourke Street; the city aglow; lights sparkle in the Paris end of Collins Street.*

CITY OF LIGHTS

This thriving cosmopolis burns brightly at night when the city's many distinct entertainment sectors come to life. The city itself is aglow as the restaurants and hotels, theatres and clubs switch on for the evening's entertainments. The Yarra's southern bank is transformed into a shimmering world of colour and light demanding discovery. Following the yellow-lit roads radiating out to Melbourne's inner city districts will lead to a whole new menu of options from the busy modern Italian style and clamour of Lygon Street, Carlton, to the upmarket eateries of South Yarra, and beyond.

Clockwise from top: *The glow of the curved facade of the Crown Entertainment Complex tower dominates the Southbank precinct; Flinders Street Station and its dome are brilliantly lit; twilight's soft light paints the city and the Yarra; lights enhance Simon Rigg's sculpture* The Guardians *on Southbank Promenade.* **Opposite:** *Neon lights up the city.*

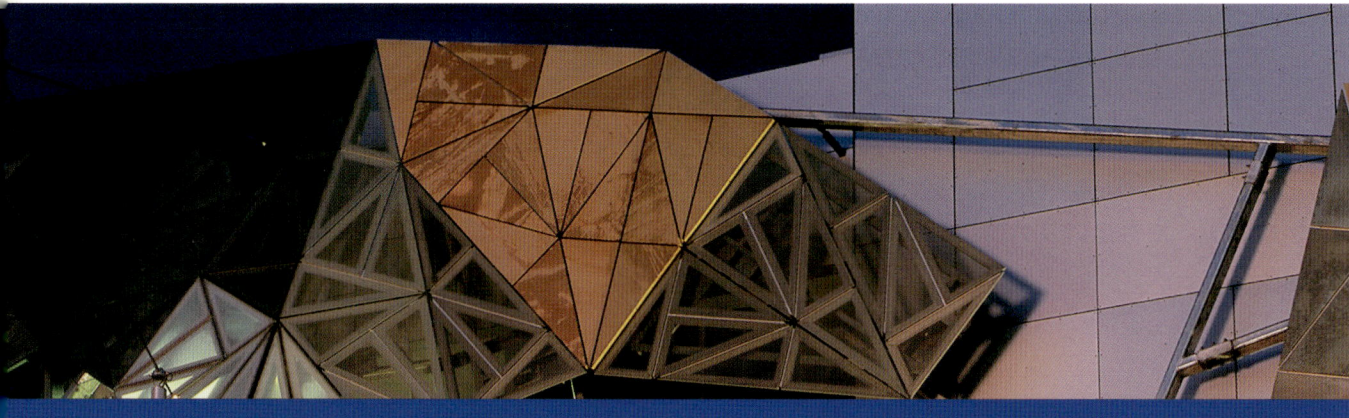

ON THE YARRA'S BANKS

Where some rivers divide, Melbourne's Yarra unites. It connects the city with its Indigenous past, merges green spaces and bay with big city bustle, bridges eras and brings together a city's people in a fusion of culture, colour and celebration.

The Yarra's powerful role belies its modest origins as a meeting of rivulets and streams far to the city's north. Where sturdy bridges now stand, punts and ferries once conveyed Melbourne's early inhabitants across the river. Over time its eccentric course has been straightened to prevent flooding. Now – with such developments as the calming parklands of Birrarung Marr and the startling architectural energy of Federation Square – this is truly a river of re-invention.

The Yarra has been the setting for some of Melbourne's most festive moments, including the annual Moomba Waterfest. The development of the Yarra's southern bank beyond historic Princes Bridge has seen the river undergo a remarkable renaissance. At Southgate an extensive plantation of public art has taken root and flourished alongside open-air cafés and restaurants. Further along Southbank Promenade, the leisure attractions of Crown Entertainment Complex and Casino co-exist with the restored 1885 Irish barque *Polly Woodside*, a sentimental memento of Melbourne's early port days.

In many ways the meandering history of the Yarra River is the story of the city of Melbourne.

These pages: The bold and intriguing face of Federation Square on the Yarra's northern bank.

LIGHT AND SHADOW

As dusk casts its veil of softening light, the parks and waterways of Melbourne become places of ethereal beauty. Flanked by green borders, the waters of the Yarra reflect a glimmering twin city as it flows gently past Federation Square under the Princes Bridge toward Southgate and the bay.

To the Yarra's original inhabitants, the Wurundjeri people, the river was known as *Birrarung*, translated as "river of mists and shadows". On the Yarra's northern bank, the parklands of Birrarung Marr honour the area's Indigenous heritage.

Left: *The pastel hues of dusk deepening to night reflected in the Yarra.*

Bridging the Yarra's Banks

As the Yarra River nears the end of its 242-kilometre journey from Mount Baw Baw to Port Phillip Bay, the city's bridges reach out to span its waters. Linking St Kilda Road with the CBD is the Princes Bridge, opened in 1888. Beyond the arched footbridge at Southgate, the dual pillars of Bolte Bridge soar majestically out of the Yarra.

Clockwise from left: Three views of the footbridge from *Southgate to Flinders Walk; Princes Bridge, the gateway to Southbank Promenade and Melbourne's cultural mecca.*
Right: The 140-metre-high Gateway Towers of Bolte Bridge.

A Rower's Retreat

In the first half of last century, Melbourne's annual spring rowing regatta, the Henley-on-Yarra, was the city's biggest sporting and social event, attracting up to 300,000 people. Today, the city's major rowing clubs still operate from their traditional location on the south bank of the river in view of Federation Square. While for many the Yarra's peaceful waters offer an opportunity for quiet recreation, the river has long provided a training ground for Australia's Olympic champions in the sport.

These pages: The Yarra provides rowers with perfect conditions within sight of the towering city. The balance and rhythm of rowing, from the solitary sculler to the octopus-armed eights, have moved people to poetic and philosophic heights. To quote Kenneth Grahame's Wind in the Willows, "'Nice? It's the only thing,' said the Water Rat solemnly, as he leant forward for his stroke. 'Believe me, my young friend, there is nothing – absolutely nothing – half so much worth doing as simply messing about in boats.'"

FEDERATION SQUARE

Since its opening in 2002, the spectacularly angled geometry of Federation Square has overcome divided public opinion to become Melbourne's favourite destination. Its emphatically modern architecture was the result of a major international design competition. Constructed on the Yarra's northern bank over railway lines leading to Flinders Street Station, Federation Square now constitutes the city's most distinctive landmark.

These pages: *The distinctive textured surfaces of Federation Square glow in the twilight.*

Federation Square combines generous public space with important cultural centres, restaurants and galleries. Behind the striking fractal mosaic of sandstone, glass and zinc are housed The Australian Centre for Moving Image (ACMI), the National Design Centre and the Ian Potter Centre: NGV Australia, the largest collection of Australian art in the world.

These pages: Now a popular rendezvous point, the open spaces of Federation Square can accommodate 20,000 people. The Square's modern lines are in juxtaposition with the ornate, Moorish style of the nearby Forum Theatre on Flinders Street.

MELBOURNE AQUARIUM

Perched on the Yarra's edge at Kings Bridge, the Melbourne Aquarium is a contemporary underwater zoo offering a fascinating window on marine life. Visitors to the aquarium take a journey of discovery over three levels, including a stunning walk-through oceanarium where creatures of the deep glide by at fin's reach.

The aquarium features the life of the Southern Ocean while providing a rich panorama of Australia's many diverse marine environments, including a floor-to-ceiling coral atoll and its residents. An Ocean Theatre provides an entertaining and educative experience for sea-lovers of all ages. Glass-bottomed boat tours, shark feeding sessions and even an indoor billabong present captivating interactive insights into the aquatic habitat.

*Left, top and bottom: Visitors delight in the vibrant colours of an underwater world. **Above, top to bottom:** The modern, eye-catching aquarium is opposite the Crown Entertainment Complex on the Yarra River; the Aquarium's lights reflect in the calm waters of the river.*

Above: *Deep sea creatures at close range in the oceanarium tunnel.* **Left:** *The beautiful but venomous lionfish.*

MELBOURNE MARITIME MUSEUM

Permanently moored outside the Melbourne Exhibition Centre on the Yarra near Spencer Street Bridge, the faithfully restored tall ship *Polly Woodside* is the jewel of the Melbourne Maritime Museum. Once designated "the prettiest barque ever built in Belfast", the tri-masted coal carrier found final rest in Melbourne after plying its trade between Europe and South America, and in Australasian and Pacific waters.

The original wooden walled dry dock that is now her home once serviced and repaired ships visiting Melbourne's bustling port. Inside the heritage-listed cargo sheds is exhibited a treasure-trove of maritime artefacts, models and photographs chronicling the port's rich history.

These pages: The Polly Woodside, *a barque built in Belfast in 1885, now takes pride of place in the Melbourne Maritime Museum.*

Celebrating Southgate

Melbourne's celebration of its riverbank locale finds colourful expression at Southgate, a shopping, dining and entertainment precinct. Immediately south of Princes Bridge and enjoying a panoramic vista of Flinders Street Station and the city skyline, the area is a magnet for cheerful crowds of locals and visitors.

Art is everywhere – pavement and performance artists, sculptures and soundscapes provide a visual feast. Southgate is also the departure point for sightseeing vessels and water taxis touring the river and ferrying passengers to Melbourne's Docklands and beyond.

Right: *Southgate is the place to eat, promenade and be entertained.* **Far right:** *Street performers delight the crowds at Southgate.*

Top and above right: Alfresco diners at Southgate watch the world go by and, in turn, are watched by the passing parade. *Above and right:* Decorative street lamps on Princes Bridge; Simon Rigg's twin sculpture The Guardians on Southbank Promenade.

Right: The Yarra's banks are an exhibition space for stunning works of sculpture, such as Shearwater by Inge King. *Far right:* An intriguing bronze creation. *Below:* Deborah Halpern's eye-catching Ophelia welcomes visitors to Southgate.

YARRA'S SOUTHBANK AT NIGHT

At night Southgate's restaurants fill with diners and the colours of Southbank Promenade are transformed by inventive illumination. A short stroll by the Yarra leads to the glittering sight of the Crown Entertainment Complex. Here, the terraces are outdoor art galleries, punctuating the riverbank walk with evocative public sculpture. Playful water features and fire-breathing pillars welcome guests to this sophisticated entertainment precinct. Within lie a casino, restaurants and shops bearing the signature creations of some of the world's most exclusive designers.

*Above left to right: Art and entertainment exist side by side; an urban forest on Southbank Promenade. **Left:** Fairy lights twinkle in trees throughout the city.*
***Following pages, left to right:** Gas flares add a dramatic touch to the Crown Casino and Entertainment Complex on the Yarra's bank; a dancing light and water show at Southbank.*

AROUND THE BAY TO MORNINGTON PENINSULA

Following the gentle curve of Port Phillip Bay away from the city provides pleasures of a different nature.

The inner bayside suburbs south-east of Melbourne are linked by a single strand of sandy beach stretching from Port Melbourne to Brighton. While St Kilda's past is colourful – and at times shady – arty culture and chic cosmopolitan living collide to create one of Melbourne's most fascinating and popular locales. At Brighton the pleasures may appear more sedate, but vivaciously decorated, historic bathing boxes at Dendy Street beach give the desired address a seaside flavour all of its own.

However here the bay is only just beginning to show its true colours. The Mornington Peninsula, dividing Port Phillip Bay from Bass Strait and Westernport is a long-favoured holiday region. Melburnians migrate south to the peninsula's ocean and bay beaches in summer to immerse themselves in the pleasures of sun, sand and surf. The villages of Sorrento and Portsea are densely populated with holiday houses, flats, hotels and camping grounds meeting the perpetual demand for seasonal relaxation.

At the peninsula's end, windswept Point Nepean has a colourful history, serving as a quarantine station and fort first established in the 1800s to protect the Port of Melbourne. This important site is of natural and historical significance and is protected as a national park.

Left: Painted bathing boxes, a legacy of nineteenth-century beach culture and highly sought-after, provide a decorative backdrop at Brighton, one of Melbourne's most popular bayside suburbs.

WILLIAMSTOWN

Historic Williamstown, located at the mouth of the Yarra on the western side of Hobsons Bay, was once the main sea port of Melbourne. The busy waterfront retains a seaside village atmosphere and is awash with maritime culture. The restored facades of shops, hotels, restaurants and cafés gaze out past the bobbing masts of yachts to the bay beyond. Visitors come to Williamstown to explore and play while residents enjoy a relaxed pace of life only a few kilometres from the city.

This page: Williamstown, once Melbourne's port, is now a pleasant bayside suburb and a popular place for a walk, cycle or sail – or a refreshment break at the Anchorage Restaurant at Parsons Marina. *Opposite:* Offering safe moorings for all manner of watercraft, Williamstown's marinas are at the head of Port Phillip Bay.

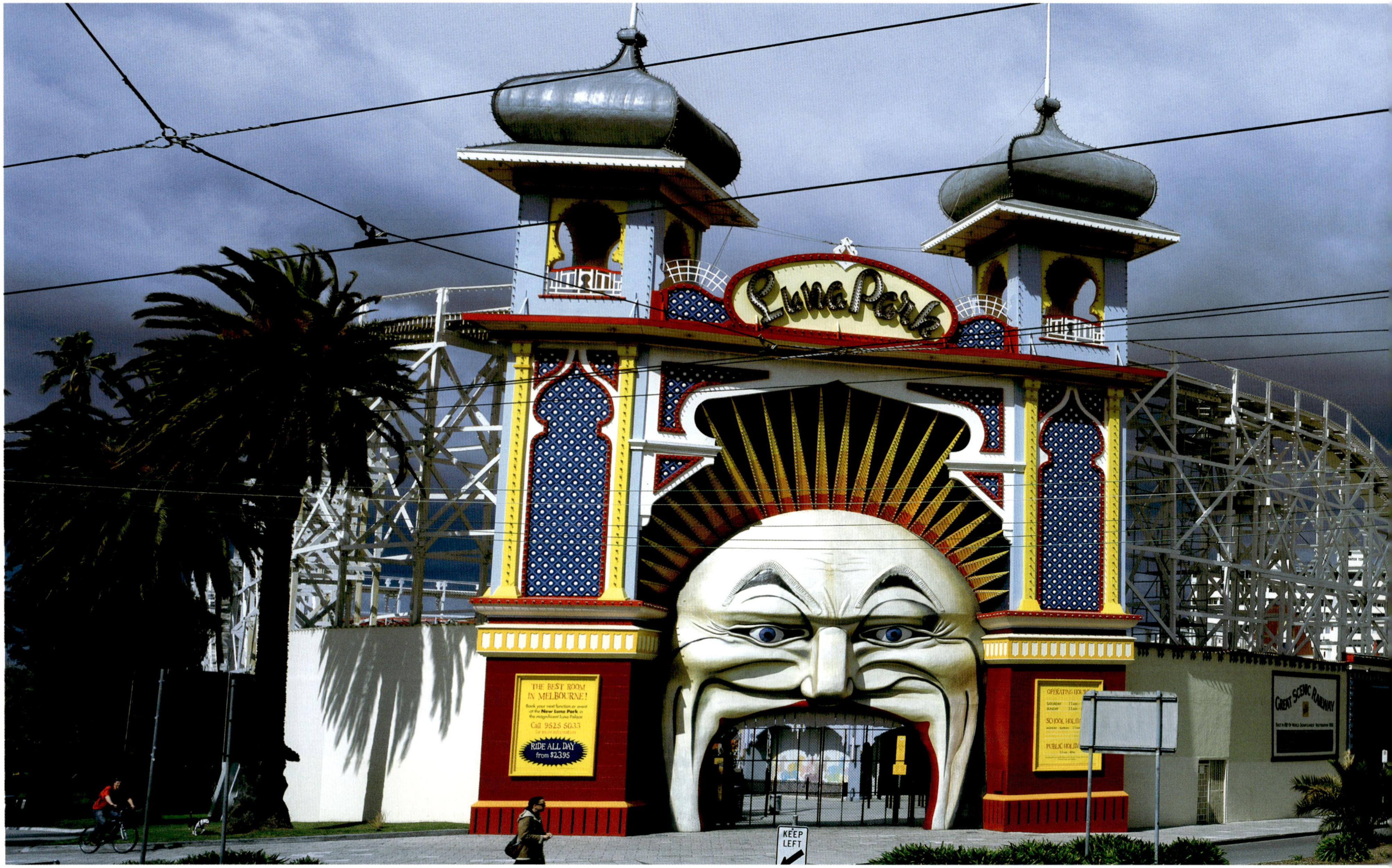
Luna Park
THE BEST ROOM IN MELBOURNE!
Book your next function or event at the New Luna Park in the magnificent Luna Palace
Call 9525 5033
RIDE ALL DAY from $23.95
GREAT SCENIC RAILWAY
KEEP LEFT

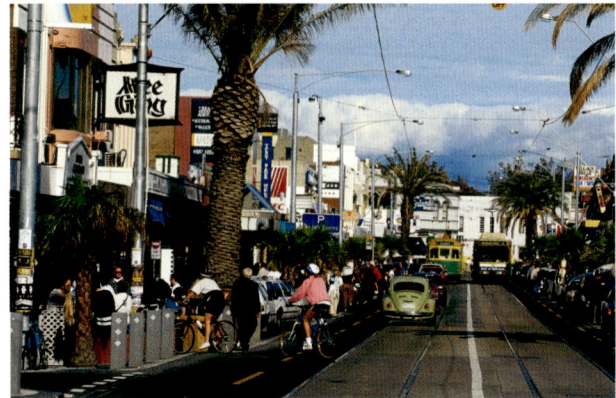

St Kilda – Bayside Suburb of Many Faces

Melbourne's most famous bayside suburb, St Kilda, has undergone a rebirth that evokes its history as both fashionable seaside retreat and bohemian enclave. Picturesquely situated on the shores of Port Phillip Bay, St Kilda is now an energetic centre of cultural activity, boasting numerous music venues, theatres and art galleries. Along the Upper Esplanade, craft markets draw crowds of Melburnians and beachside visitors. On Acland Street, traditional European cake shops provide a mouthwatering taste of the suburb's multicultural heritage. At the entrance to one of Melbourne's best loved icons, Luna Park, a giant laughing face invites all to enjoy the nostalgic pleasures of a traditional amusement park. By evening, Fitzroy Street, St Kilda's main thoroughfare, is abuzz with visitors to its popular bars and restaurants.

Above: Luna Park and the adjacent Palais Theatre have entertained and entranced visitors to St Kilda since early last century.
Left: Busy Acland Street attracts many weekend visitors to graze at its smorgasbord of multicultural food.

ST KILDA PIER

Jutting out into Port Phillip Bay from St Kilda Beach, this grand old wooden pier was first constructed in the 1850s to assist early settlers to receive provisions and timber. The original kiosk, which graced the pier's southernmost point for 99 years, was long part of St Kilda's soul. The building was destroyed by fire in 2003, leaving just memories of Australia's only kiosk on a pier. It was once the arrival point for royal yachts and later a dance hall for American soldiers during World War II. From St Kilda Pier ferries and charter boats lure passengers for Williamstown and tours of the remarkably urban Little Penguin colony on St Kilda Breakwater. The pier also gives shelter to a flotilla of yachts. Fishing from the pier's landings and rocks continues to be a popular pursuit.

Left: *Twilight at St Kilda Pier.*
Above: *Sailing into the sunset off St Kilda Pier.*

Point Nepean

Colloquially known as "Quarantine", the windswept promontory of Point Nepean at the far tip of Mornington Peninsula was once home to a quarantine station servicing inbound shipping. Here, where Port Phillip Bay meets the wilds of Bass Strait, still stands an old fort, Melbourne's erstwhile wartime guardian.

Above: An aerial view of Point Nepean. Far left: A moment of reflection on one of the jetties dotted throughout Port Phillip Bay. Left: The rotunda at Sorrento. Opposite: Jetties abound in the coves of the Mornington Peninsula.

CAPE SCHANCK

At the southernmost point of Mornington Peninsula, the Cape Schanck Lighthouse has been a welcome sight for sailors since 1859. To the west, spectacular coastal views may be had in Mornington Peninsula National Park and to the north the Cape is overlooked by Arthurs Seat State Park. The beaches to the east offer sunbathing and great surfing.

Left: Cape Schanck and the lighthouse. *Top:* The chairlift at Arthurs Seat. *Above:* The peninsula's beaches are a holiday playground for Melburnians.

WEST OF MELBOURNE

Journeying west from Melbourne, one is reminded at every turn of nature's determining hand.

Visitors to Werribee's Open Range Zoo encounter some of the world's wildest species. On the Bellarine Peninsula's surf coast, some of Australia's biggest waves buffet the shore. At Point Lonsdale, a vital lighthouse protects vessels against the turbulent violence of Port Phillip Bay's notorious Rip.

Further south, the panoramic Great Ocean Road closely traces the tightly winding curves of Victoria's coast, a feat made all the more remarkable by the steep fall of the Otway Ranges to the ocean. The road was constructed after World War I by returned servicemen without the aid of heavy machinery and their labours have granted a legacy of astonishing beauty. From Anglesea to Apollo Bay, the coast road delivers ever-changing, magnificent seascapes.

Turning inland to the Otway Ranges reveals wonders to equal the coast's delights – rainforest, waterfalls and towering trees. But nature's exhibition has only just begun. Beyond Port Campbell, wind and wave have conspired to create divine art, using the limestone cliffs as the sculptor's rock. The resulting stone stacks, cut by erosion from the coast and battered by ocean swells, provide one of the world's great spectacles.

This unforgettable reminder of nature's power is a fitting prelude to the Shipwreck Coast, the torturous stretch of Southern Ocean leading to Warrnambool and Port Fairy that claimed many a ship and crew over centuries past.

Opposite: Split Point Lighthouse, nicknamed the "White Lady" stands guard over the popular ocean beach retreat, Aireys Inlet. ***Above left:*** *The scenic Indented Coast.*

WERRIBEE PARK MANSION AND OPEN RANGE ZOO

Once Victoria's largest private residence, Werribee Park Mansion is a restored 60-room Italianate home built in the 1870s and set amidst extensive formal gardens. The estate formed part of 93,000 acres of prime pastoral land and was home to wealthy Scottish settlers and their servants and workers. From 1923, the Mansion functioned as a seminary for 50 years before being purchased by the Victorian government. Part of surrounding Werribee Park was set aside for Werribee Open Range Zoo. Today, the Zoo's authentic recreation of the habitat of African, Asian and American species provides a breathtaking experience. Here zebras, giraffes and rhinoceroses wander the savannah, bison browse the prairie and hippos luxuriate at an African waterhole.

Above: Werribee Park Mansion is surrounded by landscaped gardens, an ornamental lake and a natural riverine area.
Left: Gazelles and zebras cavort at the Werribee Open Range Zoo.

Clockwise from top left: Woolstore; a tableau of shearers at the National Wool Museum; Mark Stoner's *North* sculpture on the Waterfront; Eastern Beach; Cunningham Pier.

GEELONG

Victoria's largest provincial city, Geelong lies 72 kilometres south-west of Melbourne on the waters of Corio Bay. The Wathaurong people occupied the area before European settlement in 1835 and the name Geelong derives from *jillong*, an Indigenous word translated as "place of the sea bird over the white cliffs". Geelong's many heritage buildings, wharves and woolstores illustrate the city's history as a major port serving Melbourne and Victoria's rural western district. On the waterfront more than a hundred statues created by sculptor Jan Mitchell from local pier timbers vividly bring Geelong's past to life, including representations of a Wathaurong family, the explorer Matthew Flinders and a military band. Geelong is also the gateway to the beach resorts of the Bellarine Peninsula and spectacular vistas of the Great Ocean Road.

Top left: Cunningham Pier on the Geelong waterfront. ***Above and top right:*** Jan Mitchell's Baywalk Bollards trail.

At the Mouth of the Bay

The pretty seaside villages and resort towns dotted along the Bellarine Peninsula, once an important grain growing region, are now tourism, fishing and watersport centres. The prodigious waves sweeping into Bells Beach and Jan Juc have made them world-famous surfing destinations. At peninsula's end, Point Lonsdale Lighthouse alerts vessels to the perils of the infamous Rip, renowned as one of the most treacherous bay entrances in the world. Below the lighthouse lies a small cave, which purportedly once gave shelter to William Buckley, an escaped convict who lived among the Wathaurong people for more than thirty years prior to European settlement.

*Above: Point Lonsdale Lighthouse. **Left:** Fishing and swimming at Queenscliff. **Above right:** Windsurfers take advantage of the stiff breeze.*

TO THE GREAT OCEAN ROAD FROM QUEENSCLIFF

Historic Queenscliff forever holds a place in Victorian's hearts with its quaint guesthouses, restored boutique hotels and fine dining. The nineteenth-century charm of sandstone buildings and cottages adorned with cast-iron lacework provides a relaxed seaside atmosphere redolent of bygone days.

Overlooking the bay from Shortlands Bluff is Fort Queenscliff, built to protect shipping lanes from attack in the 1850s. Today the old fortification remains replete with cannons, guardrooms, cells and even a dry moat. The unique Black Lighthouse is built from Scottish cut bluestone.

But not all is of the past. From Queenscliff Harbour, a modern twin hull ferry transports visitors and their vehicles to Sorrento across the bay.

These pages: Queenscliff is a historic resort town providing a relaxing seaside getaway for city-dwellers.

Clockwise from above: The Black Lighthouse at Fort Queenscliff; nineteenth-century houses; Seaview House; Hotel Royal.

Top left and above: *Split Point Lighthouse at Aireys Inlet keeps watch over the turbulent Bass Strait waters.*
Left: *Houses cling to the steep hillside that sweeps down to the beach.*

Left: Lorne, on the Great Ocean Road and nestled between the Otway Ranges and the waters of Loutit Bay, is a highly popular tourist resort. **Above:** Lorne Pier marks the start of the famous Pier to Pub open water swimming event.

Top to bottom: Carved wooden sculptures and outdoor furniture are a feature of the Apollo Bay foreshore; Apollo Bay seen from Mariner's Lookout; boats moored at Apollo Bay. **Opposite:** Cape Otway Lighthouse was the longest continuous operating lighthouse on the Australian mainland until decommissioned in 1994. Today a low-powered solar light operates in front of the tower.

THE OTWAY RANGES

The rugged escarpments, plunging waterfalls and temperate rainforests of the Otway Ranges form a spectacular backdrop to the Great Ocean Road from Anglesea to Cape Otway. Stretching north to Colac's volcanic plains, the ranges support vast forests of Messmate, Manna Gum, Myrtle Beech and towering Mountain Ash. Near Triplet Falls, a 600-metre-long elevated walkway known as the Otway Fly offers the chance to stroll among the treetops and survey the surrounding beauty from a 45-metre-high lookout.

Left: Hopetoun Falls. ***Above:*** Erskine Falls. ***Right:*** Otway Ranges rainforest.

NATURE AS SCULPTOR

Carved over millennia by the relentless wind-whipped waves of the Southern Ocean, the Twelve Apostles are arrayed along a 32-kilometre stretch of the Great Ocean Road designated as Port Campbell National Park. These hauntingly beautiful limestone "orphans" and their neighbouring cousins London Bridge, Mutton Bird Island and the Bakers Oven are perhaps Victoria's most awe-inspiring natural features. Continuing erosion has seen the original twelve now reduced to just eight.

Along the coast, stubborn fingers of rock jut into the ocean, forming a series of wind protected coves accessible by boardwalks and tracks. Wooden platforms erected on the heathland provide perfect vantage points and on these beaches nesting Little Penguins may be seen at dusk and dawn.

Top: *Two of the Twelve Apostles.* **Right, top to bottom:** *Apostles Lookout; cycling the Great Ocean Road.* **Opposite:** *London Bridge, once connected to the mainland but now severed by nature's force.* **Following pages:** *Some of the many moods of the Twelve Apostles.*

ANCIENT MARINERS

The call of the sea is always close along the Shipwreck Coast. From the busy provincial centre of Warrnambool to the fashionably sleepy fishing village of Port Fairy, this is a region steeped in maritime lore that values and preserves its heritage. Shipwreck sites abound, as do tales of survivors and lost souls.

Clockwise from top left: Proudfoots Hopkins River Boathouse at Warrnambool; surfboards at Anglesea; a wooden dinghy overlooked by Lady Bay Lower Lighthouse; Lady Bay Upper Lighthouse; Port Fairy of olde-world charm.

This page: Beautiful beaches and harbours surrounded by prime grazing land typify the region.

THE GRAMPIANS AND MOUNT ARAPILES

Known as *Gariwerd* to Indigenous Australians, the Grampians are a series of dramatic sandstone ranges rising out of the flat wheatfields of western Victoria. Many of the rock formations within the Grampians National Park are central to Indigenous people's creation beliefs and the area contains more than two-thirds of Victoria's Aboriginal art sites. Long a popular bushwalking, climbing and camping destination, the Grampians are home to more than 800 species of flora as well as abundant birdlife including waterbirds, raptors, parrots and songbirds. Significant populations of kangaroos, wallabies, echidnas and Koalas also reside within these ancient lands. For the vertically inspired, the extreme angles and sheer drops of nearby Mount Arapiles offer Australia's most challenging rock climbing routes.

Left: *A climber enjoys the challenge of Mount Arapiles.*
Below: *Camping is permitted in the Grampians.*
Right: *Eastern Grey Kangaroos frequent the camp sites.*
Opposite: *Mackenzie Falls, Grampians National Park.*

EAST OF MELBOURNE

It is a mark of Melbourne's easy accommodation with its natural environment that a wealth of native wildlife prospers in close proximity to the city.

Less than an hour's drive east of the CBD, the gracious ranges, fern gullies and pristine waterways of the Dandenong Ranges provide a home for more than 200 species. In Sherbrook Forest, kookaburras, lyrebirds, bellbirds and rosellas produce a symphony of birdsong.

In the Yarra Ranges, Healesville Sanctuary is also home to more than 200 species of native wildlife living in their natural habitats. Its staff is dedicated to the care and conservation of native species including Platypus, Koala, echidna and Dingo in Healesville's 31 hectares of bushland. This world-class fauna park provides extensive opportunities to observe and learn about some of Australia's fascinating creatures.

The traditional pilgrimage to Westernport's Phillip Island to see Little Penguins returning to shore after a hard day's fishing rightfully remains on most visitors' itineraries. But the island also offers the rare chance to sight Australian Fur-seals and visit a unique Koala Conservation Centre where wooden walkways climb high into the Koala's eucalypt habitat.

These attractive, distinct, yet complementary regions east of Melbourne combine to create an Eden for Australia's native creatures.

Above left: Rhododendrons are a feature of gardens in the Dandenong Ranges. Opposite: Although settlement has largely displaced fruit growing and cattle raising in the beautiful districts east of Melbourne, some pockets of verdant grazing country remain.

Above: Puffing Billy *transports visitors into the Dandenong Ranges and another age.* **Left:** *Masterful representations of Indigenous peoples at the William Ricketts Sanctuary.* **Opposite:** *The floral beauty of the internationally renowned National Rhododendron Garden in Olinda spreads over 43 hectares.*

DANDENONG RANGES

Only 50 kilometres east of Melbourne, the rejuvenating forests, gardens and glades of the Dandenong Ranges are a haven for Australian flora and fauna. Whether viewed from the carriages of restored steam train, *Puffing Billy*, or one of the many walking tracks, the Dandenongs are a favourite Melbourne retreat. At Olinda, the marvel of the National Rhododendron Gardens is only matched by the imitative talents of its most vocal resident, the Superb Lyrebird.

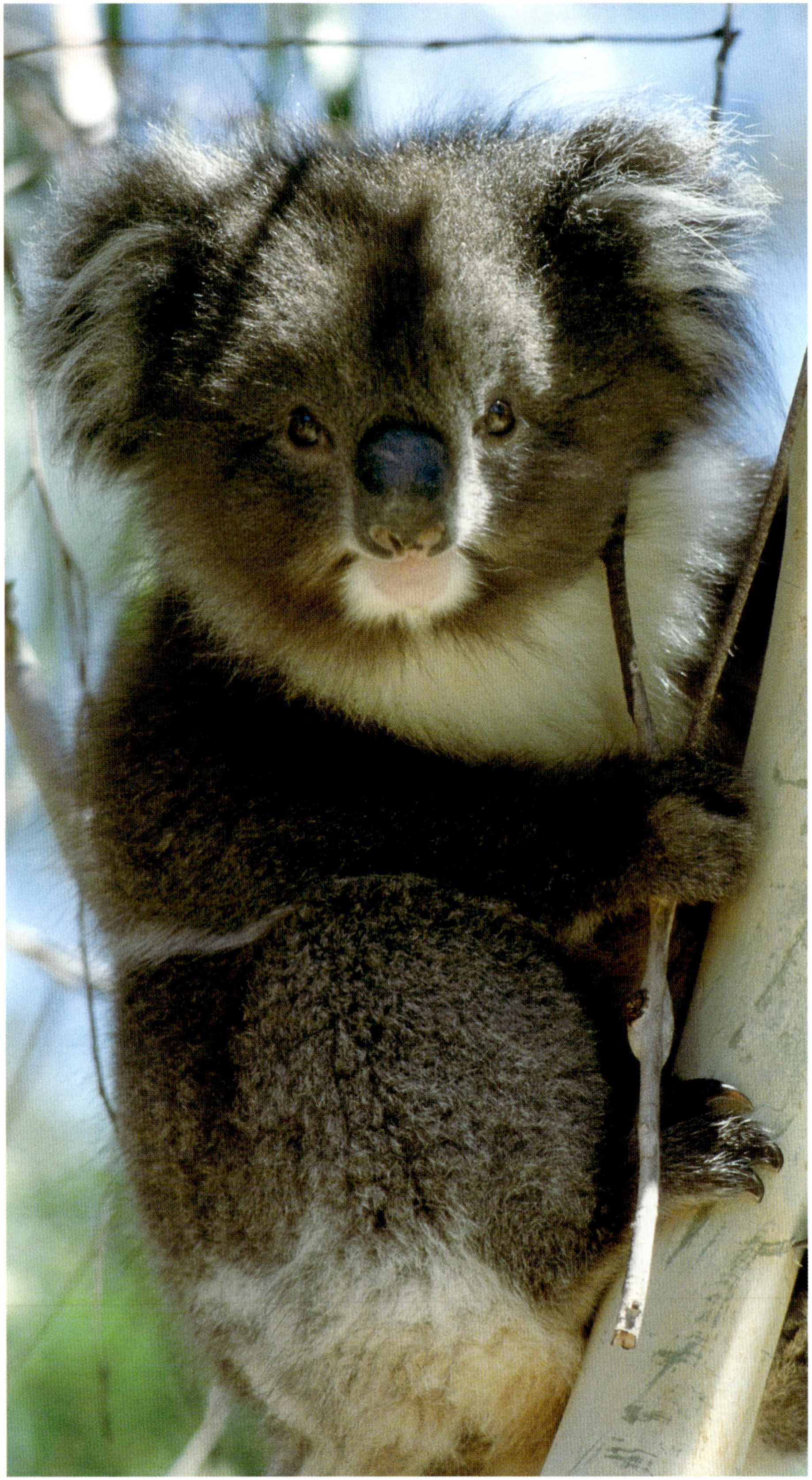
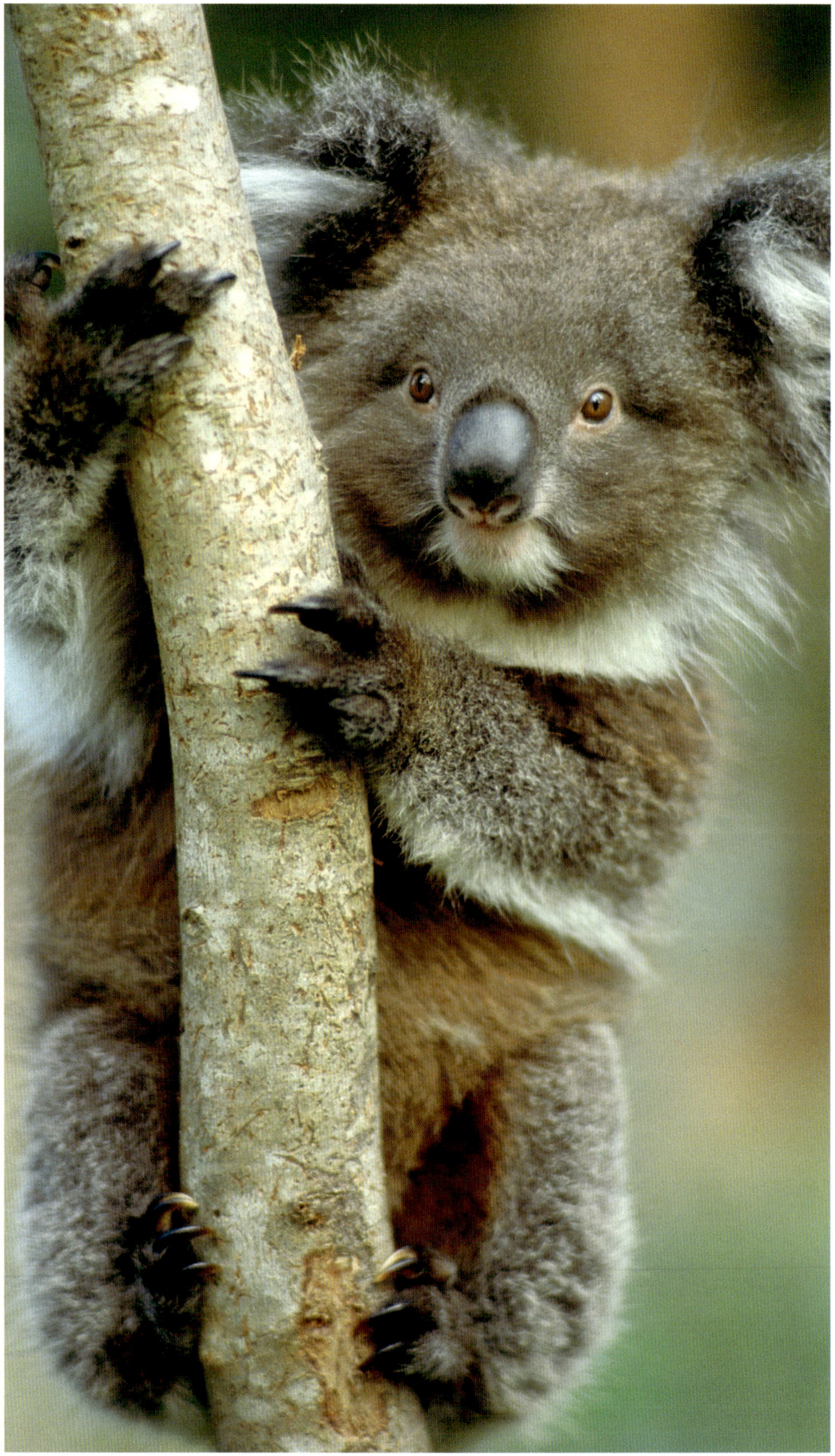

HEALESVILLE SANCTUARY

Home to bears that are not bears and egg-laying monotremes bearing duckbills, Healesville Sanctuary is an Australian wildlife centre like no other. Set in bushland east of Melbourne, the sanctuary offers the opportunity to observe the habits and idiosyncrasies of some of Australia's most elusive native creatures at close range. Focusing on research, conservation and education, Healesville provides insights into a rarely seen world.

Opposite: *Tilly the Koala, as a youngster (right) and an adult (left), was very popular with visitors to the Sanctuary.* **Clockwise from right:** *Keeper and Koala; Dingo; Short-beaked Echidna; Platypus.*

Until Healesville Sanctuary's world-first success in the 1940s, the breeding of Platypuses in captivity was long considered impossible. In fact, it was another 55 years before that event would be repeated, this time with twins. In 2000, another baby Platypus was born. The success of Healesville's program reflects the sanctuary's precise replication of the Platypus's native creek habitat and conditions. The extraordinary Platypusary at Healesville reveals the hitherto hidden world of the mysterious monotreme.

THE ENCHANTED FOREST

The Yarra Ranges National Park is a vital catchment for Melbourne's water supply. Home to more than forty species of mammal, including the endangered Leadbeater's Possum, the Mountain Ash forests, and temperate rainforests and fern gullies of the national park stretch north and west from Healesville.

Clockwise from top left: The eucalypt forests and fern gullies of the Yarra Ranges; the Superb Lyrebird is found here; Crimson Rosellas are also common; walking tracks traverse mossy streams into lush forest.

Autumn in the Yarra Ranges

In autumn the turning leaves of vast stands of trees suffuse the ranges with glorious colour. At Mt Donna Buang's summit there are panoramic views of Melbourne and the Dandenongs, and deciduous trees burnish the vistas. As autumn turns to winter, snowfalls provide good runs for tobogganing and cross-country skiing. The trees lose their leaves, and the winter sun filters through the branches.

This page: Oaks, beeches, and poplars clothed in the saffron, scarlet and russet hues of autumn.

PHILLIP ISLAND

Two hours' drive south-east of Melbourne at the entrance to Westernport Bay, Phillip Island is connected to the mainland by bridge and to visitor's hearts by its famous Little Penguin colony and its Koalas. The island is popular for its protected beaches on the bay side and its surfing beaches on the ocean side. The main town of Cowes is the centre for commerce and of the café and restaurant scene.

The island enjoys a booming ecotourism industry and visitors flock to Summerland Beach to watch the penguins emerge from the ocean at sunset and march up the beach to burrows in the dunes to feed their young. Further around the coast at the Nobbies, Australian Fur-seals swim, sprawl and socialise on the rocky ocean outcrops within view of an especially designed public observatory.

Throughout the year the island's focus turns to motorsports. The big bikes roar on the famous Grand Prix Circuit at the World Superbike Championship in April and the Australian Motorcycle Grand Prix in October. In November comes the non-stop action of the V8 Supercar Championship.

Phillip Island's birdlife is a source of fascination to visitors.
Clockwise from top left: *Silver Gulls flock in hope of scraps of food; Australian Pelicans come in to be fed at San Remo; Little Penguins trek to their burrows.*
Opposite and following pages: *Windswept coastal heath, rocky shores and outcrops and turbulent seas are the hallmarks of the island's coasts that front Bass Strait.*

INDEX

Published by Steve Parish Publishing Pty Ltd
PO Box 1058, Archerfield, Queensland 4108 Australia

www.steveparish.com.au

© copyright Steve Parish Publishing Pty Ltd

ISBN 978174021735 4
10 9 8 7 6 5 4 3 2

Photography: Steve Parish

Photographic Assistance: Ian Roberts pp. 8-9, 32, 42 left, 52 top, 58 bottom, 59, 66 middle, 70, 72 bottom right & 77.

Additional photography: p. 6: Courtesy Historic Photographs www.historicphotographs.com.au; p. 25: Pat Slater; p. 30: Rodney Start, Museum Victoria; p. 31 bottom: Jon Augier, Museum Victoria; p. 34 right: Tourism Victoria; p. 44: Tom Putt, Sport the Library; p. 45: Jeff Crow, Sport the Library; p. 48 top: Sport the Library/Presse Sports; p. 66 top left & bottom left, & p. 67: Courtesy of Melbourne Aquarium; p. 123 bottom: Hans & Judy Beste.

Front cover: Melbourne City on the banks of the Yarra River. Back cover, top to bottom: Flinders Street Station; Jan Mitchell's Baywalk Bollards at Geelong; London Bridge.

Publisher: Donald Greig
Text: Rod Howard
Editing: Kate Lovett; Michele Perry & Karin Cox, SPP
Design: Cristina Pecetta & Gill Stack, SPP
Production: Tiffany Johnson; Tina Brewster, SPP

Prepress by Colour Chiefs Digital Imaging, Brisbane, Australia
Printed in China by PrintPlus Limited

**Produced in Australia at the
Steve Parish Publishing Studios**

online

FOR PRODUCTS
www.steveparish.com.au

FOR LIMITED EDITION PRINTS
www.steveparishexhibits.com.au

FOR PHOTOGRAPHY EZINE
www.photographaustralia.com.au